KREMLIN

Steve Goldsworthy

www.av2books.com

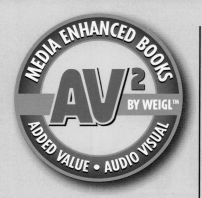

AV² provides enriched content that supplements and complements this book. Weigl's AV² books strive to create inspired learning and engage young minds in a total learning experience.

Your AV² Media Enhanced books come alive with...

Audio
Listen to sections of the book read aloud.

Key Words
Study vocabulary, and complete a matching word activity.

Video
Watch informative video clips.

Quizzes
Test your knowledge.

Embedded Weblinks
Gain additional information for research.

Slide Show
View images and captions, and prepare a presentation.

Try This!
Complete activities and hands-on experiments.

... and much, much more!

Go to **www.av2books.com**, and enter this book's unique code.

BOOK CODE

B158818

AV² by Weigl brings you media enhanced books that support active learning.

Published by AV² by Weigl
350 5th Avenue, 59th Floor
New York, NY 10118
Website: www.av2books.com   www.weigl.com

Library of Congress Cataloging-in-Publication Data

Goldsworthy, Steve.
  Kremlin / Steve Goldsworthy.
     pages cm. -- (Virtual field trip)
  Includes index.
  ISBN 978-1-62127-464-3 (hardcover : alk. paper) -- ISBN 978-1-62127-470-4 (softcover : alk. paper)
  1. Kremlin (Moscow, Russia)--Juvenile literature. 2. Moscow (Russia)--Buildings, structures, etc.--Juvenile literature. I. Title.
  DK602.3.G55 2013
  947'.31--dc23

                    2012046538

Printed in the United States of America in North Mankato, Minnesota
1 2 3 4 5 6 7 8 9 0 18 17 16 15 14 13

032013
WEP280213

Editor: Heather Kissock
Design: Terry Paulhus

Every reasonable effort has been made to trace ownership and to obtain permission to reprint copyright material. The publishers would be pleased to have any errors or omissions brought to their attention so that they may be corrected in subsequent printings.

Weigl acknowledges Getty Images as its primary image supplier for this title.

Contents

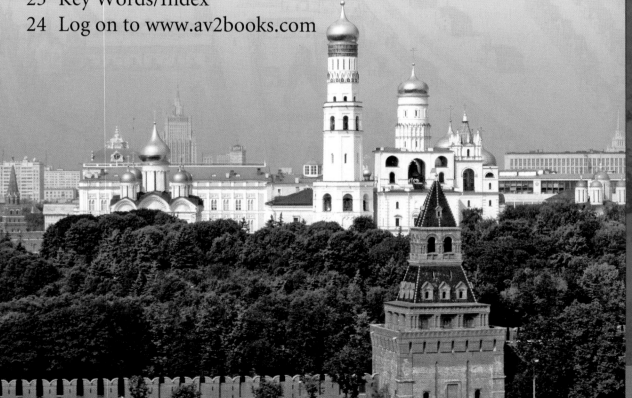

What Is the Kremlin?

Located in the heart of Moscow, the Kremlin serves as the center of Russian government. It stands as a symbol of the country's past as well as its present. This **fortified** city has stood on the site for centuries, weathering the victories and tragedies of the country.

The word *kremlin* is Russian for "fortress." Before the city became fortified, it sat on open land and was vulnerable to attack. Over time, a wall was built around the city to protect it. Several towers along the wall served as **sentry** posts. From this high vantage point, soldiers could scan the distance for any threats to the city's security.

The walls and towers provided the protection the city needed to grow. The Kremlin wall and towers now surround palaces, cathedrals, and government buildings. These structures showcase the beautiful **architecture** of Russia. They represent several different eras of Russian history as well.

In the past, the Kremlin was home to Russian **tsars**, emperors, and empresses, from Ivan the Terrible to Catherine the Great. Today, the Kremlin houses the official residence of the president of the Russian Federation. To many, the Kremlin also refers to the government of the Russian Federation itself.

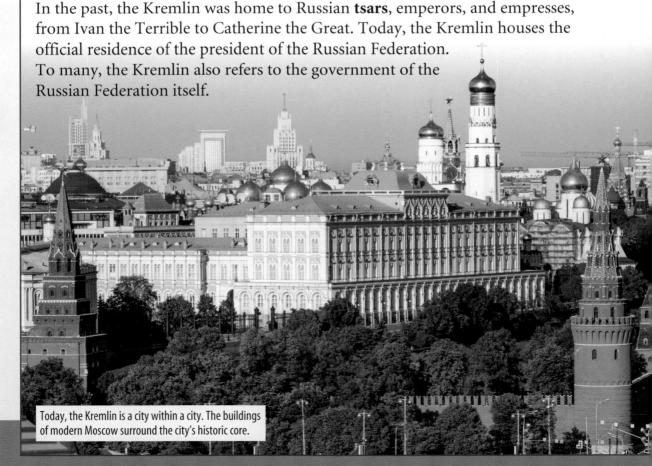

Today, the Kremlin is a city within a city. The buildings of modern Moscow surround the city's historic core.

Snapshot of Russia

Russia is a country in northern Eurasia. Covering 6,601,700 square miles (17,098,200 square kilometers), it is the world's largest country. Due to its immense size, Russia shares borders with several countries. To its west lie Norway, Finland, Estonia, Latvia, Lithuania, and Poland. Belarus, Ukraine, Georgia, Azerbaijan, and Kazakhstan sit to the southwest. China, Mongolia, and North Korea lie to the south.

INTRODUCING RUSSIA

CAPITAL CITY: Moscow

FLAG:

POPULATION: 143,300,000 (2012)

OFFICIAL LANGUAGE: Russian

CURRENCY: Russian ruble

CLIMATE: Humid continental, with large seasonal and regional differences

SUMMER TEMPERATURE: Average of 75° Fahrenheit (24° Celsius)

WINTER TEMPERATURE: Average of 7°F (−14°C)

TIME ZONE: Coordinated Universal Time (UTC)

Russian Words to Know

When visiting a foreign country, it is always a good idea to know some words and phrases of the local language. Practice the phrases below to prepare for a trip to Russia.

Pozhaluysta
You're welcome

Privet
Hello

Spasibo
Thank you

Vy govorite po angliyski?
Do you speak English?

Da
Yes

Skol'ka eto stoit?
How much is this?

Menya zovut...
My name is

Izvinite!
Excuse me

Vy mozhete mne pomoch?
Can you help me?

Nyet
No

Kak dela?
How are you?

Kak vas zovut?
What is your name?

A Step Back in Time

Buildings have stood on the Kremlin site since at least the 1100s. Prior to the Kremlin's construction, the site was home to a royal hunting lodge. Over time, a town began to form around the lodge. To protect the town and its residents, walls were built around it. The town continued to grow. By the middle of the 15th century, Moscow was the **seat** of the Russian territory.

In 1462, Ivan the Great became grand prince of Russia. As Moscow was his official residence, he wanted the city to reflect its royal status. He set to work rebuilding the Kremlin, constructing new buildings and upgrading older structures.

CONSTRUCTION TIMELINE

1156 AD
Prince Yuri Dolgoruky fortifies the city of Moscow.

1475
Ivan the Great begins to construct and reconstruct the Kremlin.

1485 to 1495
New walls and towers are built by Italian **master** architects.

1613 to 1676
Tsar Mikhail Romanov and his son Alexis add several buildings to the complex.

1712 to 1736
Peter the Great moves the royal court from Moscow to St. Petersburg. The Kremlin falls into disrepair.

The city of Moscow erected a statue of Prince Yuri Dolgoruky in 1954 to honor its founder. It stands in front of the mayor's office.

The changes Tsar Mikhail Romanov and his son m to the Kremlin were recorded in a 1663 map, wh believed to be one of the first maps of the compl

The final result was so grand that Moscow remained the center of Russian rule for almost 300 years, until Peter the Great, another Russian tsar, shifted the power to St. Petersburg. However, in 1918, following the **Russian Revolution**, the government set up its headquarters at the Kremlin. The Kremlin has been Russia's seat of government ever since.

Vladimir Lenin was one of the key political thinkers behind the Russian Revolution. Following the revolution, he became the first leader of the newly created Soviet Union.

1773
Empress Catherine the Great orders the demolition of several of the Kremlin's churches and palaces to make room for her new residence at the Kremlin.

1776 to 1787
Russian architect Matvey Kazakov reconstructs sections of the Kremlin.

1837
Architect Konstantin Thon constructs the Grand Kremlin Palace by order of Tsar Nicholas I.

1946 to 1951
The Kremlin walls and **battlements** are restored.

1955
The Kremlin is opened to the public.

Catherine the Great ruled Russia from 1762 to 1796. She is best known for expanding the Russian Empire and revitalizing the country.

Restoration projects continue to take place throughout the Kremlin. The Cathedral of the Annunciation received an upgrade in 2008.

The Kremlin's Location

The Kremlin is situated on the top of Borovitskiy Hill, right next to the Moskva River. A European people called the Vyatichi settled on this spot in the 11th century. It was considered a good location for many reasons. Its elevation provided the Vyatichi with a superior vantage point. They were able to see a great distance across the plain and prepare early for any threats from aggressors. Being next to the river was also of benefit. The Moskva River was a source of water, food, and transportation.

Prince Yuri Dolgoruky recognized the value of the river when he built his fort on the hill in 1156. The fort weathered many invasions and attacks over the years, but its people were always able to repair and rebuild. This was, in large part, because of the river. Supplies and manpower could be brought quickly to the site. The ability to rebuild in an efficient manner kept the settlement from being defeated for long. As a result, people continued to live there.

The Moskva River continues to be an important transportation route and water source for Moscow.

The Kremlin Today

The Kremlin has undergone many changes over the years. Several churches and cathedrals have been torn down or replaced. Other buildings have stood in the complex for more than 500 years. Today, the Kremlin serves two key roles. Part of the complex has been set aside for the Russian government. The remaining areas form a series of museums and historic sites. More than one million tourists visit the Kremlin every year to gain perspective of Russia's past and present.

Area The Kremlin covers an area of 2.96 million square feet (275,000 sq. meters).

Height The tallest building in the Kremlin is the Ivan the Great Bell Tower, at 266 feet (81 m) in height.

266 feet (81 m)

7,332 feet (2,235 m)

Wall Lengths The walls that surround the complex are 7,332 feet (2,235 m) long.

Kremlin Buildings

The Kremlin has housed all levels of church and state in Russia. Many of its buildings reflect these interests. Other buildings showcase an amazing collection of Russian art and culture.

Armory Once a storage area for military weapons, the Armory now houses one of Russia's most important museums. Nine halls of gallery space display everything from ceremonial dress worn by tsars and priests to treasures, weapons, and royal carriages.

The Armory is Moscow's oldest museum. Its display space features more than 4,000 artifacts.

The Great Kremlin Palace is the largest building inside the Kremlin. It covers almost 269,098 square feet (25,000 sq. m).

Great Kremlin Palace Built to be the tsar's official residence, the Great Kremlin Palace features several luxurious rooms and grand halls. One of the most spectacular is the Andreyevsky Hall, also known as the throne hall. Most important state ceremonies are held in this hall. Its walls are covered in golden chains and blue fabric. Ten bronze chandeliers hang from the ceiling. Three thrones sit on a platform at the end of the hall.

The interior of the Terem Palace features elaborate artwork.

Terem Palace The Terem Palace is part of the Great Kremlin Palace complex. Prior to the construction of the Great Kremlin Palace, it was the residence of the tsar and his family. The building has three tiers, with a golden-roofed *terem*, or tower chamber, at the top. This level housed the tsar's personal rooms.

The Senate is one of the youngest buildings in the Kremlin. It was built between 1776 and 1788.

Kremlin Senate The Kremlin Senate is the most important government building in the Kremlin. It is the working residence of the president of Russia. The Senate has a triangular shape that surrounds a courtyard. Inside, the building features a large, circular hall called the rotunda. It is about 82 feet (25 m) in diameter and 89 feet (27 m) high.

Ivan the Great Bell Tower For more than 400 years, the Ivan the Great Bell Tower was the tallest building in Moscow. Its height was eventually surpassed by modern buildings. The tower is accompanied by a four-story **belfry**. Together, these two buildings house 21 bells.

The Ivan the Great Bell Tower has a museum and an observation gallery.

Cathedral of the Assumption The oldest and most important church in the Kremlin, the Cathedral of the Assumption is the seat of the Russian Orthodox Church. It was here that Russia's tsars and emperors were crowned. The building's exterior is plain, but the interior houses several religious **icons** and **frescoes**.

VIRTUAL TOUR

Only some of the Kremlin buildings are open to the public. People can visit the museums on their own, but need to book special tours of the palaces. Government buildings are not for public viewing.

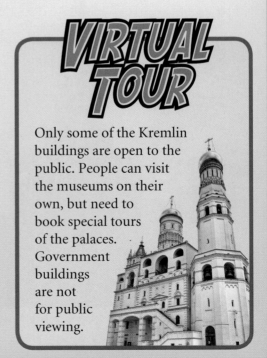

Following the Russian Revolution, the Cathedral of the Assumption became a museum. Today, it operates as both a church and a museum.

Kremlin Features

The Kremlin has a variety of structures, monuments, and quiet spaces. Some have a definite function. Others pay tribute to the country's history. A few add to the beauty of the site.

Walls The Kremlin walls create the triangular shape of the city. Their height varies as they follow the curve of Borovitskiy Hill. In some places, the walls are as high as 62 feet (19 m). In others, they are only 16 feet (5 m) high. A walkway extends along the top of the walls. It is up to 13 feet (4 m) wide in some areas.

The present Kremlin walls were built between 1485 and 1495. The work was supervised by Italian architects.

The Troitskaya Tower is the main entrance to the Kremlin. Most tourists and visitors enter the Kremlin through its gate.

Towers Twenty towers are placed strategically along the Kremlin's walls. In the past, they served as watch posts for the soldiers who guarded the fortress. Each tower varies in shape and size, but all of them are topped with a green roof. The oldest tower is Tainitskaya, built in 1485. The last tower built, Tsarskaya, was constructed in 1680. The tallest tower is the Troitskaya, or Trinity, Tower. It is 262.5 feet (80 m) tall.

Monuments Two unique monuments can be found on Ivanovskaya Square. The Tsar Bell is the world's largest bell. **Cast** in 1735, it is more than 19 feet (6 m) tall and 19 feet (6 m) wide, and weighs 202 tons (183 tonnes). Close by sits the Tsar Cannon. Built in 1586, the cannon barrel is more than 16 feet (5 m) long and features elaborate carvings.

A large piece of the Tsar Bell broke off during a fire in 1737. It sits beside the rest of the bell.

Together, the Taynitsky and Grand Kremlin Gardens form an urban park inside the Kremlin.

Gardens The Kremlin has a few green spaces sprinkled throughout the site. One of the best-known is the Taynitsky, or Secret, Garden. This small garden runs along the Kremlin wall, leading toward the Moskva River. The Grand Kremlin Garden sits on the upper part of the Taynitsky Garden. This garden leads toward Ivanovskaya Square.

Squares Many of the Kremlin's buildings were constructed around a central plaza, or square. Cathedral Square is the very heart of the Kremlin complex. It is surrounded by a number of churches and cathedrals, including the Cathedral of the Assumption. The largest square is the Ivanovskaya. The Ivan the Great Bell Tower sits to the side of this square.

Due to the many churches that surround it, Cathedral Square was often the site of grand religious processions and parades.

Big Ideas behind the Kremlin

The Kremlin underwent many changes over the years. Some of these changes were structural, using new materials and construction methods to create a stronger structure. Other changes were undertaken to make the Kremlin more attractive.

The distance between the towers was determined by weapon range. As the south side of the Kremlin was more vulnerable to attack, the towers there were built closer to each other.

Fortress

As a fortress, the Kremlin was built to protect its citizens. The people who designed it had to consider the weapons that would threaten the structure. The first Kremlin walls were made of wood. They served as a barrier to invaders who arrived on foot and used hand-held weapons. Stone walls were built with the arrival of **missile** weaponry, such as catapults. These walls were better able to withstand the force of large rocks hitting them. When guns became the weapons of choice, the stone was changed to brick, and more towers were built. The high towers protected the city from cannon fire and allowed more soldiers to be stationed along the Kremlin wall.

Russian Revival Architecture

As Moscow rose in stature, Russian rulers began changing the Kremlin's appearance to reflect its importance to the country. Some of the buildings currently in the Kremlin were built during the reign of Nicholas I. They reflect a style of architecture called Russian Revival. This type of architecture has both Russian and **Byzantine** influences. One of the key designs used in this style is the "onion dome," which is used to top many Russian churches and cathedrals. The dome is an example of traditional Russian architecture. Another feature is the use of **vaults**. These are found in many Byzantine structures.

Onion domes are usually larger in diameter than the base on which they sit.

Science at Work in the Kremlin

The people who built the Kremlin did not have power tools to help in the construction process. Instead, they used simple machines to help ease their workload. Simple machines make a hard job easier by using scientific principles.

A pulley was used to lift the Tsar Bell from its casting pit.

Pulleys

During the construction of the Kremlin, pulleys were used to lift stone and other materials into place. A pulley is a wheel with a groove around the edge. A rope is run along the groove. Pulling on one side of the rope causes the wheel to turn. This moves the other end of the rope in the opposite direction, allowing a heavy load to be lifted more easily. Pulleys make lifting easier because they work with **gravity**. Instead of pulling heavy construction materials up toward them, workers pull down on the rope to lift the materials. Pulling down is easier than pulling up, so the job could be completed faster and with less strain on the workers.

Wheels and Axles

When the construction of the Kremlin's stone walls began, the rock had to be brought from nearby quarries. This was done using carts and wagons. These vehicles use wheels and axles to move across the ground. The wheel and axle is a two-part simple machine. Wheels

The wheel and axle helped move construction materials from one site to another in a quick and efficient manner.

rotate, so they reduce the **friction** between the moving object and the ground. The axle is the structure that attaches the wheel to the rest of the cart. By using carts with wheels and axles, people could move large loads of stone. Even carts full of stones would move easily along the ground because of the reduced friction.

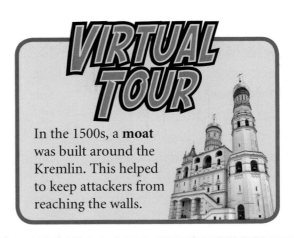
VIRTUAL TOUR

In the 1500s, a **moat** was built around the Kremlin. This helped to keep attackers from reaching the walls.

The Kremlin Builders

The design and construction of the various buildings within the Moscow Kremlin took place over centuries. From tsars to architects to laborers, it took hundreds of people to build these structures.

Ivan the Great was the first Russian ruler to use the title of tsar.

Ivan the Great Grand Prince of Russia, 1462–1505

Ivan III Vasilyevich was born January 22, 1440 in Moscow, Russia. He became one of Russia's longest reigning leaders. Ivan ruled the Grand Duchy of Moscow. The center of this state was the Moscow Kremlin. When Ivan the Great decided to rebuild the Kremlin, he wanted the buildings to reflect the artistry of the Italian **Renaissance**. He hired Italian artists and architects to plan the new buildings. Ivan the Great oversaw the construction of many of the Kremlin's best-known buildings, including the Ivan the Great Bell Tower.

Aristotele Fioravanti
Architect

Aristotele Fioravanti was an Italian architect and engineer. In 1474, Ivan the Great called on him to build one of the most magnificent structures in

The Cathedral of the Assumption's vaulted ceilings feature elaborate and colorful frescoes.

the Kremlin—the Cathedral of the Assumption. Fioravanti traveled to Russia to study traditional Russian methods of design. He wanted an open and spacious design for the cathedral in the Kremlin. The cathedral's five-dome design and vaulted ceilings were very popular. They inspired many other churches and cathedrals throughout Russia. The crowning of Russia's first tsar, Ivan the Terrible, took place in this cathedral in 1547.

Konstantin Thon Architect

Konstantin Thon was an official architect in Russia in the 1800s. Emperor Nicholas I hired Thon to oversee the construction of the Great Kremlin Palace in 1837. Nicholas wanted his palace to celebrate the greatness of Russian rule and not be a showcase for the Italian architecture. Thon

Thon was also a teacher. He taught architecture at Moscow's Imperial Academy of Arts.

was chosen because he was known for designing buildings that had a Russian style. Nicholas was so impressed with the imposing Grand Kremlin Palace that he gave Thon the job of designing the Kremlin Armory.

Architects

An architect is a person who designs and plans buildings, and then supervises their construction. The architects who designed the Kremlin buildings had to consider a number of factors. They had to understand the purpose of the building and how it was to be used. This information allowed them to design rooms and other spaces. The architects also had to understand construction techniques and building materials so that they could create a building that was structurally sound. Many of the Kremlin's architects studied architecture in Italy and France under the masters of the day before taking on their own projects.

Architects draw blueprints of their building plans. These drawings help everyone understand how the building will be set up.

Masons

The construction of the Kremlin involved the work of specialized builders called masons. Masons are people who work with stone or brick. The Kremlin required both types of masons at different points in history. When the original wooden walls were removed, masons were hired to build stone walls. This required cutting stone into blocks and setting them in place. When Ivan the Great decided to renovate the Kremlin walls, masons were brought in to lay the brick and build a sturdy structure.

Brick masons arrange the bricks in rows called courses. They use mortar, a type of paste, to bond the bricks together.

Laborers

General laborers were hired to help with the rebuilding of the Kremlin. Like today's construction workers, laborers played a key role at the construction site. They put the materials into the hands of the people who needed them. They did this by carrying the materials on their shoulders and loading them onto carts. Laborers also helped lift and position materials into place.

Laborers continue to play an important role in construction. They take materials to the work site and operate equipment.

Similar Structures around the World

Fortified cities can be found in many parts of the world. There are even other kremlins in Russia. Most of these walled cities were built during the **medieval** era. Like the Moscow Kremlin, they were constructed as a way to protect citizens from invading forces.

Kazan Kremlin

BUILT: Begun in 1556
LOCATION: Kazan, Republic of Tatarstan, Russia
DESIGN: Various, under Ivan the Terrible
DESCRIPTION: Like the Moscow Kremlin, the Kazan Kremlin has many magnificent buildings. The Annunciation Cathedral takes its name and design from the Moscow Kremlin's Annunciation Cathedral. The cathedral bell tower was modeled after the Ivan the Great Bell Tower. The city is surrounded by walls and many towers. It houses the biggest **mosque** in Europe, the Qolsharif Mosque, which opened in 2005. The Kazan Kremlin was declared a **UNESCO World Heritage Site** in 2000.

The Qolsharif Mosque stands on the site where the region's principal mosque stood in the 1500s.

Taroudant

Taroudant's walls can appear to be pink, orange, red, brown, or gold, depending on the time of day and the position of the Sun.

BUILT: 1500s
LOCATION: Taroudant, Morocco
DESIGN: Mohammed ash-Sheikh
DESCRIPTION: Taroudant is a city in southern Morocco, known best for its markets. The city's red earth walls were constructed as a defense against European invaders. The walls extend almost 3.7 miles (6 km) and have 19 **bastions** and 130 towers strategically placed within them. Taroudant is said to have the best-preserved town walls in the country.

Carcassonne

BUILT: Sixth century BC
LOCATION: Carcassonne, Aude Province, France
DESIGN: Various
DESCRIPTION: Carcassonne was an important trading center in the sixth century and has been a walled city since at least 330 BC. The walls have been rebuilt at various points in history. They are made up of two separate lines that extend for about 1.8 miles (3 km). The walls seen today are a combination of Roman and medieval influences. The city underwent a major restoration in the 19th century, when the walls and historic buildings were in danger of ruin. Carcassonne was named a UNESCO World Heritage Site in 1997.

The restoration of Carcassonne began in 1846 and was not completed until 1910.

Old Quebec's walls feature four main entrances, including the St. Louis Gate.

Quebec City

BUILT: 1608
LOCATION: Quebec City, Quebec, Canada
DESIGN: Samuel de Champlain
DESCRIPTION: Quebec City is the only remaining fortified city in North America north of Mexico. Its walls encircle Old Quebec City, which was originally a French settlement. The city's first walls consisted of only 11 towers linked by **palisades**. However, as the French and English battled for control of the area, the walls became taller and stronger. They were renovated further when the English took over the city in the late 1700s. Today, the walls remain intact, and four of the original gates still stand.

Issues Facing the Kremlin

The Kremlin's walls, towers, and buildings are hundreds of years old. They were built using the best materials of the time. However, the passage of time has created problems for these structures. Many are experiencing wear due to their age and the environment in which they stand.

WHAT IS THE ISSUE?

Acid rain is damaging the towers, walls, and other structures found within the Kremlin.

The interiors of the buildings are being affected by humid air, exposure to light, and age.

EFFECTS

Metal roofs and monuments are **corroding**. Stonework throughout the complex is experiencing wear.

Paintings are fading. Wall paint is chipping. Furniture upholstery is wearing.

ACTION TAKEN

Structures that are at risk have been cleaned and treated with an anti-corrosion coating. Sections or parts that are beyond repair have been replaced.

Restoration projects are ongoing. Experts from all over the world are brought in to clean paintings, restore furniture, and fix problems related to air quality.

Tower Building

The Ivan the Great Bell Tower is one of the best-known structures in the Kremlin. Follow the instructions below to build your own version of the Ivan the Great Bell Tower.

Materials
- paper towel tube
- white paper
- scissors
- glue
- black marker
- gold ball Christmas ornament
- tape
- small bell
- string

Instructions

1. Begin by cutting the white paper so that it will wrap neatly around the paper towel tube. Once cut, glue the paper around the tube.

2. Use the black marker to draw windows on the paper covering the tube.

3. Attach a small piece of string to the bell, and tape it to the Christmas ornament.

4. Slip the bell into the tube until the ball rests on top of the tube. Glue the ornament to the top of the tube.

5. Enjoy ringing the bell in your bell tower!

Kremlin Quiz

Q What does the word *kremlin* mean?

A It is Russian for "fortress."

Q When was the first fortified settlement built on the site of the Kremlin?

A Yuri Dolgoruky built a fort there in 1156.

Q Who was responsible for the first large-scale renovation of the Kremlin?

A Ivan the Great

Q What is the tallest building in the Kremlin?

A The Ivan the Great Bell Tower, at 266 feet (81 m) in height

Key Words

acid rain: air pollution produced when acid chemicals are incorporated into rain, snow, fog, or mist

architecture: the art and science of designing and constructing buildings

bastions: projecting parts of a fort

battlements: notched openings at the top of walls through which weapons are aimed

belfry: a bell tower that is attached to another building

Byzantine: relating to the eastern part of the Roman empire

cast: set in a mold

corroding: eating or wearing away

culture: the artistic and social pursuits, expressions, and tastes valued by a society

fortified: strengthened and secured with walls and other defensive structures

frescoes: wall paintings

friction: a force that slows down motion when surfaces slide against each other

gravity: the force that moves objects toward the center of Earth

icons: pictures or statues of religious people

master: an artist of great and exemplary skill

medieval: a time in history between the fifth and fifteenth centuries

missile: an object that is forcibly propelled at a target

moat: a deep wide ditch, usually filled with water, surrounding a fortress or castle as a protection against attack

mosque: a place of worship for those who follow the Muslim faith

palisades: fences made of stakes

Renaissance: a style of art and architecture developed between the 14th and 16th centuries, with emphasis on classic styles of art

Russian Revolution: a 1917 uprising that caused the ousting of the Russian tsarist regime

seat: a center of authority

sentry: a soldier who is guarding a given spot

tsars: the male heads of the ruling Russian royal family

UNESCO World Heritage Site: a site designated by the United Nations to be of great cultural worth to the world and in need of protection

vaults: an arched form used to make room for a ceiling

Index

Log on to www.av2books.com

AV² by Weigl brings you media enhanced books that support active learning. Go to www.av2books.com, and enter the special code found on page 2 of this book. You will gain access to enriched and enhanced content that supplements and complements this book. Content includes video, audio, weblinks, quizzes, a slide show, and activities.

AV² Online Navigation

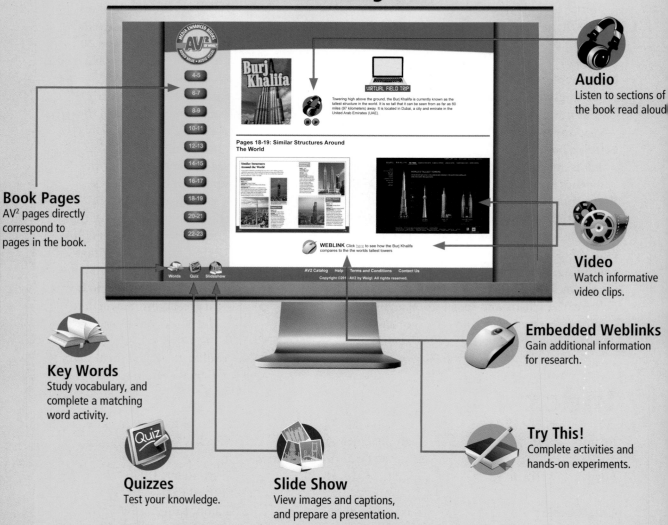

Audio
Listen to sections of the book read aloud

Book Pages
AV² pages directly correspond to pages in the book.

Video
Watch informative video clips.

Key Words
Study vocabulary, and complete a matching word activity.

Embedded Weblinks
Gain additional information for research.

Quizzes
Test your knowledge.

Slide Show
View images and captions, and prepare a presentation.

Try This!
Complete activities and hands-on experiments.

AV² was built to bridge the gap between print and digital. We encourage you to tell us what you like and what you want to see in the future.

Sign up to be an AV² Ambassador at www.av2books.com/ambassador.

Due to the dynamic nature of the Internet, some of the URLs and activities provided as part of AV² by Weigl may have changed or ceased to exist. AV² by Weigl accepts no responsibility for any such changes. All media enhanced books are regularly monitored to update addresses and sites in a timely manner. Contact AV² by Weigl at 1-866-649-3445 or av2books@weigl.com with any questions, comments, or feedback.